The Aquinas Lecture, 1970

IDEAS
AND CONCEPTS

Under the Auspices of the
Wisconsin-Alpha Chapter of Phi Sigma Tau

By

JULIUS R. WEINBERG, Ph.D.

MARQUETTE UNIVERSITY PRESS
MILWAUKEE
1970

Library of Congress Catalog Number 74-119369

SBN 87462-135-6

Prefatory

The Wisconsin-Alpha Chapter of Phi Sigma Tau, the National Honor Society for Philosophy at Marquette University, each year invites a scholar to deliver a lecture in honor of St. Thomas Aquinas whose feast day is March 7. The lectures are customarily given on the first Sunday of March.

The 1970 Aquinas Lecture *Ideas and Concepts* was delivered on March 1 in the Peter A. Brooks Memorial Union by Professor Julius R. Weinberg, Vilas Professor of Philosophy, University of Wisconsin.

Professor Weinberg was born September 3, 1908, in Zanesville, Ohio. He earned the A.B. in 1931 and the M.A. in 1932 at Ohio State University; the Ph.D. at Cornell University in 1935.

He began his teaching career at Cornell University and from 1941 to 1947 was Instructor and Assistant Professor at the University of Cincinnati. He joined the faculty of the University of Wisconsin in 1947 and was promoted to Associate

Professor in the following year. In 1953 he was appointed Professor and in 1962 received the honor of Vilas Professor of Philosophy, Institute for Research in the Humanities, University of Wisconsin.

Professor Weinberg has had an abiding interest in problems connected with human knowledge and with the History of Medieval Philosophy, especially the late medieval period, and he has written extensively in both areas.

The publications of Professor Weinberg include: *An Examination of Logical Positivism,* London: Kegan Paul, 1936, translated into Italian and Spanish; *Nicolaus of Autrecourt,* Princeton: Princeton University Press, 1948; *A Short History of Medieval Philosophy,* Princeton: Princeton University Press, 1964; *Abstraction, Relation and Induction,* Madison: University of Wisconsin Press, 1965; articles in many philosophical journals.

To those publications Phi Sigma Tau is pleased to add: *Ideas and Concepts.*

Ideas and Concepts

The subject I wish to discuss today has been thoroughly explored in its many aspects by philosophers from classical antiquity until the present day, and it is clear that a working majority of practitioners of philosophy could not be found that would agree on most of the things I shall have to say. Therefore, I would be satisfied if I succeed in my reflections in causing you to rethink whatever views you have espoused on the subject. At any rate I cannot hope to bring you to agree entirely with my criticisms of earlier views or with any positive doctrines I may appear to defend. It will be quite enough if I can cause you to review whatever views you now hold. Philosophy is a continuing search, by dialogue, for greater clarity in understanding the difficulties which beset the answers with which we tend to be prematurely satisfied to questions which are essentially different from those of the natural sciences. It is very difficult to explain in what these essential

differences consist and I shall not attempt
to do it here.

A simple way of stating my problem
would be this: Are there ideas or concepts, and are they essential to any satis-
factory explanation of human thought?
A number of philosophers have held that
the answer to these questions is plainly
affirmative. For how else can we accept
the essential distinction between thought
and other occurrences or states such as
physical processes or conditions in the
extra-cognitive departments of the world?

That there is a difference of kind between the contents of consciousness and
the denizens of the non-conscious world
has been often denied, but it seems to
me to be quite clear, and, as many if
not all of the considerations which support this contention are doubtless known
to you, I shall not attempt to rehearse
them again at this time. At any rate, I
want to make it quite clear that this is
not one of the questions I am concerned
with today.

What concerns me primarily can be

put as follows: In order to account for some of the commonest statements about what is involved in human thinking do we have to assume that to certain expressions which are the grammatical accusatives of thought-verbs, desire-verbs, and the like, single simple non-verbal but intra-cognitive items correspond? For example, do we have to assume that something of the sort corresponds to "a horse" in thought when we say, e.g. "John is (was) thinking of a horse", "John wanted a horse," or the like? Again in "He believed that a greater than God cannot exist" does something intra-cognitive have to correspond to the expression "a greater than God"? But, before we proceed to the examination of such cases, there are other apparently less controversial cases which may as well be brought to our attention here.

Consider ordinary claims to the effect that I am now perceiving a chair, a horse, or any natural or artificial object you please. Is it necessary, in order to make good sense of such statements, to assume

that there is an intra-psychic but non-verbal corrrelative of the word "chair", "horse,"
etc.? There is, historically speaking, a
great precedent for thinking that this is
the case. At the same time there are also
historical precedents for casting doubt
on such a view. And in some cases, these
opposing tendencies are found in the same
author. For one very distinguished example we have Aristotle. In *De Inter-
pretatione,* (C.1, 16a 3 ff.), he states that
written words are symbols of spoken
words and the latter are symbols for affections in the soul. In this passage, Aristotle assumes that the affections in the
soul are the same (in kind) for all men,
however much their spoken or written lan-
guages differ. This presumably because
Aristotle thinks that human beings have
generally the same sort of perceptual experiences because they live in the same
world which consists of things of the
same sorts.

Yet Aristotle also recognizes that many
words are systematically ambiguous and
so could not have referents which are

peculiar and proper to those very words. On the contrary, such words have different but somehow resembling referents in different instances of their use. I am not suggesting here that these doctrines might not somehow be reconciled, but only that if they are developed in certain ways they would lead to radically different views of the relation between language and thought.

Certainly the most influential doctrine in Western Philosophy which professed to explain this relation between language and thought is the doctrine that there are concepts or ideas which constitute a medium between the cognizing agent and the things which are known. And it is equally certain that a considerable support for this view was derived from assumptions about language, about the nature of perception, and finally about the nature of the objects of perception.

The use of the terms "Idea" and "Concept" must be explained first of all. As technical terms, *idea* and *eidos* (as well as a few others) were used by Plato to refer to Forms which were the stable and eternal meanings of common nouns or adjectives. The Forms were usually thought to be separate from the physical world, although Plato seems to vacillate on this point, because the language of "participation" suggests a degree of immanence, whilst the use of "imitation" suggests that Forms are separate from the particulars which are their copies. Since most Forms could be defined, most Forms were in some way complex. The sort of complexity which Forms have is suggested in the dialogue, *The Sophist*. If we assume that the "Greatest Kinds" are Forms, then some Forms blend with others, and so some have some internal complexity which is supposed, however, to be consistent with their unity. This doctrine of blending of Forms has, I believe, some remote affinities with the doctrine which Aristotle later brings forth regarding genus and difference. It is only the highest Form and the most specific Forms which consist of not further differentiable features. Plato never systematized his views sufficiently to enable his readers to be very sure about any of these aspects of his thought.

The critique to which the doctrine of separate Forms was subjected by Aristotle, and Aristotle's own development, involved a radical difference in the meanings of *idea* and *eidos*. For Aristotle, form (with one or more exceptions, namely, the Prime Mover or Movers and the Active Intellect) becomes a constitutive part of the physical individual. The term *eidos* is, however, employed to mean what is meant by "species" and is often used in conjunction with *genos* (i.e. "genus"). We understand what something essentially is by receiving its form in our souls without the matter of which it is the form. The unity of form and matter in composite substances is the basis of our conceptual understanding of what such a composite substance is, but it is not clearly explained how the simple presence of the form of a thing in consciousness would convey the knowledge that the form was combined in some way with matter.

For Plato, the ideas are not thoughts although the soul has the knowledge of Forms present to it by previous direct acquaintance with the Forms in its previous disembodied life. For Aristotle the knowledge of forms is effected by what some of the Medievals called *abstractio*.

By the time the medieval Christian scholastics began serious discussion of the problems of human cognition, however, the term "idea" had been pre-empted to mean "thoughts in the divine mind."[1] This had been already done by Philo and Clement of Alexandria, and by some of the pagan neo-platonists—and the usage was well-established by the fourth century in St. Augustine's writings.[2] It acquires the modern meaning given by Descartes, Locke, *et al.*, probably no earlier than the sixteenth century, first in authors like

1. It is occasionally used more broadly, e.g. by St. Thomas, but the basic meaning for the Medievals is that of exemplar.
2. *De Diversis Quaestionibus* 83, 46, 1-2.

Rabelais and Montaigne, and later by the seventeenth century philosophers.[3]

In place of the term "idea," Augustine uses a number of terms to designate the contents of human consciousness, e.g. *notio* (De Lib. Arb. II, 9, 26), *notitia* (Conf. X, 20, 29). It would require a detailed and lengthy investigation to discover the relation between a *notio* and the divine Ideas in Augustine's thought which would be impossible to develop here. It will have to suffice just to indicate a few features of his doctrine insofar as they influenced later medieval writers.

Strictly speaking, external objects do not effect changes in human consciousness since the body cannot produce changes in a spiritual substance nobler than itself. The soul by a kind of vital attention to all parts of the body notes changes in

3. There are some exceptions, however, as there usually are. Francis Mayron, for example, uses "idea" as a synonym for "quiddity" or "universal" in *Sent.* I, d.48, q.3, but he notes that the usual usage requires that ideas are only in the divine mind.

the body and impresses records of these changes upon itself. Sensation, therefore, is an activity of the soul and it produces sensory images in itself of the changes which external bodies produce on its body. There are concrete images in consciousness left from this activity. Intellectual cognition derives from some kind of illumination by the soul from the Interior Master who is always present to the soul and ready to instruct it when the soul seeks for knowledge of the laws of mathematics and of moral wisdom. Although many passages in Augustine suggest that this illumination consists in the vision of Divine Ideas, others suggest that it consists in an impression of notions of these concepts and rules by the Interior Master rather than a Malebranchean "vision of things in God." But, in any case, a doctrine of abstraction is far from any of Augustine's intentions.

St. Augustine is undoubtedly one of the many sources of the view that words stand for contents of consciousness. In *Confessions* (X, 15, 23) he assures us that

"I can name a stone, I can name the sun, while the things themselves are not present to my senses. Of course, their images are at hand in my memory. I can name bodily pain, and it is not present in me when there is no suffering. Yet unless its image were present in my memory, I would not know what I am talking about, and I would not distinguish it from pleasure in a discussion." It is true that Augustine found difficulty in explaining how the word "oblivion" or "forgetfulness" could signify anything unless we remember forgetfulness itself, and it was difficult for him to understand what this could possibly amount to, but he insisted "I am most certain that I do remember forgetfulness itself . . ." (*Conf.* X, 16, 25). It is a tribute to his genius that Augustine saw a difficulty here, and there is little point in issuing any criticism here, for the only solution that might have worked was not possibly available to him.

The doctrine of abstraction as we find it in medieval theologians of the thirteenth and later centuries had been ac-

cepted, in a simpler form, by some of
the twelfth century theologians. It under-
went some strange transformations among
some of the thirteenth century Francis-
cans who were anxious to retain as much
of the Augustinian doctrine of illumination as possible and still to use as much
as possible of the Aristotelian doctrine of
abstraction. In St. Thomas Aquinas, however, we find a genuine doctrine of abstraction which follows Aristotle as closely
as possible.

According to this account of the matter, the agent intellect abstracts an intelligible species from the phantasms received
through the senses. The concept of a
thing comes to be in the mind as a result
of the primary understanding of a thing
by means of the intelligible species. The
concept is distinct both from the mind
itself and from the intelligible species.
For its existence consists in its being
understood, whereas the existence of the
mind does not consist in its being understood. The concept is called the "word
of the intellect or of the heart" and it

is signified by the spoken word.[4] Here
again we encounter the doctrine that
words are the signs of intra-psychic contents, which, as I indicated earlier, was
one of the perennial grounds for assuming
the existence of concepts in order to explain cognitive processes. These intra-
psychic contents, both intelligible species
and the concepts consequent on the species, are described as similitudes of things.
In order to put forward some of the
principal difficulties which have been
brought against this doctrine that there
are, in thought, conceptual counterparts
to substantive words and phrases in discourse, I shall have to mention some other
doctrines of Aristotle and his medieval
followers.

First of all, the nature of a thing from
which the intelligible species is abstrac-
ed, and subsequently a concept is formed,
is always described as an essential unity
incapable of degrees. It is always contrast-

4. See especially, C. G. IV, 11; *Sum. Theol.* I,
27, 1; C. G. I, 53; *Sum. Theol.* I, 88, 2 and
2m; *De Pot. Dei*, XI, 5.

ed with accidental unities. It is contrasted with the unity of order or the unity of aggregates. It is clear, therefore, that this unity must be reflected in the conceptual counterpart of the nature of a thing existing in the world. There are, of course, composite concepts. In some sense, the concept of a particular individual will involve mention of his identifying accidents. And in the case of simple beings, i.e. spiritual substances, our concepts will necessarily be composite although their referents are not.

Let us next turn attention to the difference, usually very sharply made out, between the nature or essence of a thing and its powers. The powers are said to be consequent on the essence or to flow from the essence. This is reflected in the differences which were made out between definition and property which are discursive counterparts of the difference between essence and powers. So far as I have found, no medieval writer in the main Aristotelian tradition ever suggested that the essence was nothing but the aggregate of powers, and it is easy to see why this should be so. For such a view would be radically inconsistent with the essential unity of the nature.

A third consideration should occupy our attention for a moment. The Medievals, insofar as they followed Aristotle, held that the discovery of the essence of a thing was usually the last in order of discovery, because the human mind usually passed from what is better known to it to what was better known by nature, i.e. from the psychologically more familiar to what is logically prior. Accordingly, we must begin with the observed behavior of a thing and then infer regressively to its powers and finally to its essence. In many cases, as St. Thomas often remarked, we have to be content with knowing an aggregate of accidents, which takes the place of the essence itself.

Now let us see the bearing that all this has on the nature of concepts. In the first place, a concept which is composite in a certain respect could not adequately represent, or be a similitude of,

an essentially unified nature. If the for-
mula expressing or defining the essence
were simply a telescoped version of a
logical conjunction of formulae each expressing a power, we would have a
conjunctively complex proposition, i.e. a
conjunction of several propositions. Such
a conjunction could not be the verbal form
whose intra-psychic counterpart were a
concept of the required kind. And if
we consider that the logical constants, the
syncategoremata, were not independently
significant elements of discourse, it is difficult to see how the concept of an essence
could ever finally emerge as a unified
constituent of consciousness if the parts
of the concept were acquired gradually
in the course of investigation. At any
stage of this conceptual activity short of
its successful completion, the verbal expression of the composite concept would
suggest that its intra-psychic counterpart
were equally complex. In short, we would
be confronted with the *quid nominis,* but
not yet with the *quid rei,* with the meaning of the name of the object under

investigation, but not yet with its nature.
Now I suspect that one of the reasons
why this was not surmised by the authors
who defended the doctrine of concepts
was that the sort of logical notation which
is so readily available to us was not available to anyone before the nineteenth century. After all, the classical doctrine of
thinking, as H. H. Price called it, was
continued down through the Renaissance,
the seventeenth century, and it has sur-
vived in various modified forms to the
present time.

Some remarks on the term "concept"
are in order here. The term "conception"
is used by Boethius to express both the
intra-psychic referent of a spoken word
and of a statement, as, for example, when
he speaks of a common "conception of
the soul" (i.e. any axiom whose truth is
immediately recognized when the terms
are understood). This usage is continued
into the twelfth century by Abelard and
others. Later the term *conceptus* becomes
common. Boethius and later writers use
these terms to mean some inspectable

item of consciousness. Now it is worth-
while considering also that these concep-
tions or concepts were supposed to be
similitudes of objects outside consciousness, i.e. things in the world, and, in vir-
tue of the similarity between concepts and
objects, naturally suitable to stand for or
to represent such objects.

Doubtless, "similarity" between concepts and their extra-psychic referents is
not to be taken quite literally, a point
which some of the Greek commentators
on Aristotle had already made. But the
concrete basis of such metaphorical language tended to prejudge certain issues.
"Similarity" tends to be taken more literally in the case of a concept of a substance
than, say, a concept of an order of objects
and the order of the objects themselves.
And this, in turn, tends to enforce the
claim that the concept of a substance is
an introspectable single item of intra-
psychic experience. It is further to be
remarked that "similarity" may be a necessary condition that a represent b, it is
not a sufficient condition. And it is not

clear what additional features a concept must have in order to be a symbol for something.

The doctrine that concepts have intentional or objective existence was supposed to take care of this, but it is not clear whether or how this is so. The various explanations of intentional or objective existence of an object in thought run into difficulties at this point, and it is worth more attention than it has usually received, although recent philosophers have devoted considerable study to the question. The direction in which some of these studies has gone is to treat conceptual thinking in terms of dispositions rather than in terms of inspectable items of consciousness.[5]

One of the difficulties with interpreting all thought in terms of inspectable items of consciousness is the fact that, in some cases, the alleged item of consciousness corresponding to a noun phrase

5. See esp. H. H. Price, *Thinking and Experience*, Cambridge 1953, and *Belief*, London 1969.

would have to be ostensibly complex in the logical sense, and this would mean that we must have an acquaintance (albeit a non-perceptual acquaintance) with logical constants as items of consciousness. Some philosophers have actually maintained that this is the case, but it is difficult to see how this can be so. It would mean, I think, that when we understand a disjunctively or a conjunctively complex sentence or phrase, we are inspecting intra-psychic counterparts to "or" or to "and." It would be more plausible to give almost any other account of our ability to use logical constants.

An equally serious problem about the allegedly intentional objects is that we usually suppose that there must be such objects in order to provide referents for expressions of discourse. Thus in statements like "The present king of France exists" or "The man who broke the bank at Monte Carlo is now a pauper" it is sometimes assumed that the subject terms must have referents. But Russell has shown that such statements can be so

construed that there is no need to make
such an assumption. Moreover, in cases
in which the subject term occurs in a
statement which could not possibly be
true, it is impossible to suppose that the
subject term has a referent. Thus "The
only prime between 32 and 36 has a
rational square root", "The circle with an
area equal to that of a figure bounded by
straight lines has a diameter of 3½ meters,"
are examples. But non-mathematical examples can be given of sentences whose
subjects contain descriptive expressions
which in fact have no application. Some
modern solutions to the difficulty depend
on a different account of language in
which the so-called variables of quantifi-
cation are referring expressions which
have a significant use in context but which
neither require nor admit of inspectable counterparts in thought, but which,
nevertheless, we all understand how to
use. In order to see how such referring
expressions work, we must distinguish between the way in which nouns and descriptive predicates signify referents and

the way in which pronouns function in
a referring context. It makes some sense
to say that "John" stands for John, and
even that "red" signifies red, but it makes
no sense to say that "it" stands for it, or
that "what" or "which" stands for what
or which. Short of a philosophical inter-
pretation of modern logical theory, it
would be impossible to clarify this point
with anything like completeness, but I
believe I have provided a clue in these
examples.

Russell's theory of definite and indefinite descriptions does, I think, account for
the significance of sentences without it
being either necessary or possible to discover intra-psychic non-verbal counterparts which do not describe anything.

This theory has, of course, been at-
tacked from at least two quarters. Some
have urged that it cannot deal success-
fully with such cases as "Ponce de Leon
sought for the fountain of youth." Others
have urged that statements such as "All
John's children are asleep" have meaning

but are neither true nor false provided that John has no children.

If these objections can be sustained, it would seem to require a re-introduction of intentional objects.

I do not think that either of them has much force. The first can be dealt with somewhat as follows:

Ponce de Leon thought that "There is that which is a fountain the waters of which restore youth and that Ponce de Leon is seeking it," and he was acting in this belief by engaging in activities appropriate to holding such a belief. It is clear that we could describe in more detail what such activities would be without assuming the existence of any single intra-psychic object to correspond to "the fountain of youth." The assumption that he would have had to have concrete images in his consciousness may or may not have been true, but, in any case, contribute nothing to the purpose. For unless the images were functioning as a part of a symbolic activity they would contribute nothing to our understanding of his ca-

pacity to engage in an intelligent seeking
activity. And, in any case, the images,
qua images, could not possibly be regard-
ed as the referent of "the fountain of
youth."

The second objection (from Strawson)
requires that we adopt two policies which
inevitably conflict with one another.

Policy (1): Allow universal affirma-
tives to have a truth value only if their
subjects are instantiated, and

Policy (2): Accept, as true, whatever
follows from a truth. Now assume that
"All A is B" has a truth value because
"There are A's" is true. Also assume "All
A is B" is true. "All A is B" is equivalent
logically to "All A and C is B and all A
and not—C is B," and so "All A is B" im-
plies "All A and C is B." By policy (2),
"All A and C is B" is true. But, as we can
always choose C so that "A and C" is not
instantiated by policy (1) we should say
that "All A and C is B" has no truth-value
at all. So our policies conflict with each
other.

As far as I can see, the view that,

because declarative statements must in
any case have a meaning, they may do so
in certain cases without having a truth-
value, would require a referent for the
subject-term. But the suggestions seem
to end there and to give no account of
what such a referent could possibly be.

The objections I have suggested
against the assumption of concepts as an
explanation of human understanding were
rarely challenged in the middle ages. But
there were some developments, especially
in the fourteenth century, which suggested
other ways of explaining human cognition.

Before I turn to some of the fourteenth
century criticisms, I want to emphasize
two distinct aspects of the difficulty to
which I have called attention. One is
what may be called ontological. Essences,
in the Aristotelian-scholastic tradition, are
for the most part complex, but are not
logical complexes. An essence is supposed
to consist of discriminable parts. The way
these parts are inter-connected can be
illustrated by examples rather than explained in general terms. Consider the

relation of the generic part to its proximate difference in a specific essence. The generic part is relatively indeterminate, the proximate difference completes and determines it. Thus the kind of complexity is entirely different from any logical articulation of the constituents of a logical complex. Now we cannot make inferences about the indivisible nature of any object of discourse merely from the fact that any description we are capable of giving that object is ineluctably complex. For example, an absolutely simple object can only be described by saying that it has no parts or internally discriminable aspects. This description is logically complex but it is the only way, verbally, to characterize what is radically simple. Whether or not there are such radically simple objects is, of course, not in question. But, on the other hand, some logically complex descriptions of an object require some complexity in the object itself. If, for example, we were to say that there is an object such that the complexity of its description is a consequence of the

character of the object in the sense that
the parts of the description are deducible
from the nature of the object, there is no
way that I know to bear out such a claim
save to assume some complexity in the
object. This can be seen from the theoretical constructions of genetic theory. An
organism manifests characteristic observable features and modes of behavior. We
attempt to explain this by assuming unobservable constituents which we associate with these observable features in complex ways. We should notice that, in
addition to the axioms of logic and mathematics, special assumptions must also be
made about the unobservable constituents.
Otherwise no deduction would be possible. So I am suggesting that the burden
put upon essences in the medieval sense
is too heavy to be borne.

The application to the concepts we
have of the natures of things is plain.
There would be no way to insure the
deductive fecundity of theoretical con-
structs without the special sort of complexity I have mentioned. But this is

inconsistent with the doctrine that our
concepts are of indivisible natures and that
when they are completed they also have
the same indivisibility. In the fourteenth
century, there was a movement, largely
due to the work of Ockham, which prepared the way for a critique of concepts,
even though Ockham and many of his
successors retained the nature of the concept and made use of it in their own way.
This movement has been described as
sceptical and critical by Michalski and
others, but this characterization must be
understood in terms of the conditions in
which it arose, and of the motives of its
chief representatives. I have discussed
these matters elsewhere, and can only
mention them here. One of the founders
of the movement, perhaps the most important, was William Ockham. His writings
on philosophy and theology were composed between 1317 and 1328.

The views of Ockham can only be
understood in terms of his various disa-
greements with John Duns Scotus, and
in particular, with Scotus' doctrine of the

formal distinction. According to Scotus, there are common natures which, in themselves, are indifferent to singularity or universality. The mind can universalize such natures, and they can be contracted to existence in singular things by a contracting difference. Between this formal feature peculiar to each individual and the common nature thus contracted into singular existence there is a formal difference. This formal difference is antecedent to every operation of the mind. Yet it does not admit of any separation, that is to say, the contracted nature and the contracting or individuating difference are formally distinct, and hence distinguishable, but not separable. So the formal difference is not made by reason (i.e. not a *distinctio rationis*) nor is it a real difference, i.e. a difference which would allow one to exist without the other.

Ockham rejected this doctrine (with one exception: he allowed it in order to explain the Trinity), and he employed arguments similar to those used against the formal distinction for the purpose of denying the classical doctrine of abstraction. If two features of an individual can be distinguished, they are really different. A common nature which can be distinguished from any other feature of an individual would, in Ockham's view, be capable of really existing apart from that other feature. And any part of a concept which was distinguishable from any other part would likewise denote a real difference.

An individual substance or quality is alone real so that universality is a feature only of concepts. Concepts themselves are individual qualities of the mind, and have universality only insofar as they are capable of representing indifferently the things of which they are a similitude. Thus far, then, Ockham has a theory of concepts in many respects similar to the one I have discussed above. But when we look further we find many important differences.

The doctrine that extra-discursive things are all, if distinct, really distinct, enables Ockham to defend the plurality of substantial forms in man, and to find a real distinction between matter and form. This, of course, required an auxiliary doctrine that prime matter is actual in its own right, but this doctrine had already been championed by Henry of Ghent, Richard of Middleton, and Duns Scotus. Moreover, qualities are absolute realities and can exist, at least by divine power, apart from a substratum.

In addition to all this, Ockham was prepared to reject the doctrine of intelligible species. In its place, he maintained a direct intuitive knowledge of singulars presented to the senses. An intuitive simple (incomplex) notice of a thing can exist without knowing the causes which produced the thing or the effects which it can produce. All that a perfect simple knowledge requires is the knowledge of its constituents, i.e. its matter and form. This must not be misunderstood. Ockham denies that we can know substances of things as they are in themselves, for we have no experience of substances but through their accidents (*Quod. III*, q. 8).

Moreover, substance is known only through connotative and negative concepts such as "a being subsisting through itself," "a being not in another thing," "a being subject to all accidents" (*Sent.* I, d.3, q. 2 X). Moreover, our concepts of causal characteristics of substances are, themselves, connotative and are concepts which are obviously not simple in the sense suggested by earlier theories.

In the treatment of motion and time, Ockham moved to an even more extreme position and suggested a method which carries us far in the direction of concepts which are logically complex. He certainly does not suggest that concepts of permanent things could be so treated, even though many of his views about knowledge of substance point in the same direction. Words such as *motus, motio* have only a nominal meaning; they are, in fact, only abbreviations for prolix formulae involving many syncategorematic terms. Thus no correct concept of motion could possibly have the characteristics required of essential concepts.

The treatment of *motio* as a logical construction, more exactly, of the term *motio* as an abbreviation standing in place of a conjunction of propositions, one asserting that the mobile object is in a place, another that it is in a different place, etc., so that various incompatible predicates are successively true, was a response to theories which treated motion as a flowing form, a notion which Ockham thought could not be made intelligible. He traces the error of supposing that "motion" must have a single unique referent to the failure to recognize that different words do not always signify distinct things. Thus he says:

> From this alone, that the parts of a form are acquired in a subject one before another, such that they are not simultaneous, the motion of alteration exists. So beyond the subject and the parts of a form it is not necessary to posit any other thing, but it is sufficient to posit a subject and parts of a form such that they are not acquired at the same time.
>
> Now it may be said that this non-simultaneity is something when it is said that

the parts are not simultaneous. We must
reply that such a fabrication of abstract
nouns from adverbs, conjunctions, preposi-
tions, verbs, and syncategoremes makes
many difficulties and leads many people
into errors. For many people imagine that
just as there are distinct nouns so there are
distinct things corresponding to them, i.e.
there are as many distinct things as there
are distinct nouns. This is not the case. For
sometimes the same things are signified
when there are different, logical or grammatical modes of signifying.[6]

Moreover, Ockham insists that many definitions give only the meaning of names
and not the essences of things. Thus dis-
cussing the kinds of definitions, he argues
that those which include causes external
to the object defined are merely nominal:

Wherefore, for the meaning of Aristotle
it must be known that some definitions indicate the what of a thing whilst others indicate the what of a name. Next it must be
known that a definition can be compared
with that which is defined and with something else of which that which is defined
is predicated. Likewise, a definition in some

6. Ockham, *Tract.*, *De Successivis,* pp. 46-47.

cases is given through essential principles
(or through what state essential principles)
and this is a *formal* definition, whilst in other
cases, the definition is given through principles of some external thing and this is a
material definition.

       ✿   ✿   ✿   ✿   ✿   ✿

Definitions given through other causes
are *material,* and this is true because—fre-
quently—such definitions are given by
matter—by extending "matter" to include
anything receptive. In many cases such
definitions express the what of a name, not
the what of a thing. This can be rendered
plausible since, according to Aristotle,
"eclipse is the privation of light in the
moon from the interposition of the earth."
Now this definition expresses the (what)
meaning of a name because if the defect of
light in the moon were caused by another
cause, according to Aristotle's meaning, it
would not be called "eclipse." Likewise, if
it is laid down that thunder is caused from
the extinction of fire in a cloud, and then
called thunder, yet if a sound of the same
kind were caused in a cloud by another
cause, it would not be called thunder. So
whenever a definition is given through an
extrinsic cause, that definition only expresses the meaning of a name. This is

proved: We cannot argue from the thing
to the definition or conversely because the
thing could exist, at least by divine power,
without the extrinsic cause.[7]

I should like to turn to another critique of the view that substantive words
or phrases necessarily imply corresponding non-verbal intra-psychic counterparts.
This one is found in Gregory of Rimini
who lectured on the *Sentences* at Paris
in 1342-1344. It is an unusually brilliant
argument which is to be found in his
critique of Anselm's main argument in
chapter 2 of the *Proslogion.* As everyone
will recall, the argument has two parts:

(1) If anyone understands the phrase
*"aliquid quo majus nihil cogitari
potest,"* what is understood exists
at least in the understanding of
the hearer.

(2) If it existed only in the understanding of the hearer it would not be
that than which nothing greater
can be thought. But, as this cannot be the case, it exists both in

7. Ockham, *Sent.* I, *Prol.* q. 2.

the understanding and in reality. Gregory of Rimini only attacks part one of the argument in this critique. Anselm intends the major premiss to hold generally; it would have some such form as the following: If a substantive phrase or word is understood, its referent has at least intra-psychic existence.

Gregory shows by several arguments that this general assumption is false. Consider the first counter-instance: The expression "What is not understood" is understood. Hence, what is not understood is understood. Since the alleged conclusion is a contradiction and the premiss is consistent, the alleged conclusion does not follow therefrom.

Another argument brings out a more positive aspect of Gregory's own view. Suppose it is impossible for an ant to be bigger than an elephant. (This is Gregory's example, I shall presently supply one of my own to go with it). Then it is false to assert: "An ant bigger than an elephant can be thought." On the other hand it might very well be true to assert:

"An ant can be thought to be bigger than
an elephant."

A more modern example is the following.

It is easily proved that there are no two
integers *m, n* such that there is a prime
whose square-root equals the quotient of
m divided by *n*. So if anyone claimed that
he thought *of* or could think *of* a prime
whose square root equals the quotient of
two integers, the claim would be false.
But it would not be false to say that some-
one thought *that there is* a prime whose
square root equals the quotient of two
integers. You cannot think of what cannot be, but you can think that something
is so which in fact neither is nor could
be the case. Gregory's final counter-ex-
ample is the following:

"A greater than God cannot exist."
Now if the word "God" is replaced by the
Anselmian description "than which nothing greater can be thought" we have "A
greater than that than which nothing
greater can be thought cannot exist." Gregory states firstly, that the statement is true,

and secondly that its grammatical subject
in this case cannot have any intra-psychic
non-verbal correlate. For, as is well-known,
the Medievals did not think that anyone
could conceive what is logically absurd.
Gregory concluded that the meaning of
the sentence "A greater than that than
which nothing greater can be thought
cannot exist" must be taken as whole, and
that the grammatical subject need not, in
such negative sentences, stand for anything at all. The same applies to other
sentences like "what cannot be thought
cannot be thought." In this case, again,
the grammatical subject has no referent at
all, yet the sentence, as a whole, has a
meaning and is true.

This treatment of the question is tied
to Gregory's characteristic doctrine that
a sentence, taken as a whole, has a referent which he called "that which is signifi-
able by a sentence" or "the total significate
of a sentence," but similar treatments of
the problem can be found in other fourteenth century theologians who held no

such views, e.g. in William of Ockham and in Robert Holcot.

A considerable contribution to the critique of the classical theory of concepts was made by the extremely sceptical reflections of Nicolaus of Autrecourt. His doubts about the extent of natural knowledge led to a rejection of the conceptual system of medieval Aristotelianism, and to the substitution of the alternative and rival system of atomism. However, he explicitly rejected the claim that we can know or properly conceive the inherence-relation between substance and accidents, or between the mind and its knowledge-contents. "Those things which do not fall under the senses are not conceived . . . by proper essential concepts. So an explication can be given only according to some external similitudes" (*Exigit*, [225] 36-38).

Nicolaus' denial that substances of any kind can be known by, or validly inferred from, experience naturally led to the denial that any proper concepts of substance can be obtained. We may conjecture about the natures of extra-psychic reality, but the results will be probable at best, and the description we give will be in terms of remote analogies.

The roots of sceptical doubts about substances go very deep and they affect one's views about the nature of our conceptual capacities and accomplishments. The theory of concepts which we find in Aristotle and his successors in the middle ages was weakened by these sceptical doubts about whether we can know more than the sensible accidents of things in the world. But it must also be noticed that doubts about the maxims of causality are also intimately involved.

In the fourteenth century, such doubts were widespread, and Nicolaus of Autrecourt had a *sucèss de scandale* on a matter that was widely discussed. As is now well known, the decrees of Bishop Tempier in 1277 (the so-called *Articles of Paris*) condemned the view that "to make an accident exist without a subject has the nature of an impossibility imply-

ing contradiction."[8] Ockham had, therefore, treated accidents as absolute realities, and consequently, Nicolaus could and
did argue that no logically certifiable inference from accidents to substances could
be made save by so defining *accident* that
it entailed *having a substratum.* This
would not only have been inconsistent
with the *Articles of Paris* but would have
had merely verbal force. Nothing which
we experience of, for example, whiteness,
commits us to describing this quality as
an accident in the required sense.

If then our concept of substance is
composed of relative and negative concepts, and if logically certifiable inference
from appearances to a substantial support
is unavailable, there is no basis for the
Aristotelico-scholastic doctrine of substance. And the doctrine is further un-
dermined by Nicolaus' sceptical views of
casuality in general.

In modern philosophy in the seventeenth century, a form of the classical

8. *Chartularium Universitatis Parisiensis,* Tome
   I, Prop. 138-141.

doctrine of concepts was re-introduced in
a radically new setting by Descartes and
Locke. This time the word "idea" came
to mean for Descartes the form of any
thought, "that form by the immediate
awareness of which I am conscious of that
thought; in such a way that, when understanding what I say, I can express nothing
in words, without that very fact making
it certain that I possess the idea which
these words signify."[9] Descartes distin-
guishes between the idea as a mode of
thought and the idea as a representative
content, as he puts it, between the idea
as a formal reality and the same idea as
objective reality. This distinction was
taken from medieval authors, and Descartes probably got it from Suarez.[10] The
meaning content of consciousness must be
distinct from thought as a psychic event,
but whether there are such meaning-con-
tents as Descartes supposes, and whether

9. Descartes, "Arguments Demonstrating the
   Existence of God etc.," *Reply to Objections
   II*, H. R. II, 51.
10. Suarez, *Metaphysical Disputations*, 2, 1. 1.

the clues to which contents are objects
of consciousness can be taken from the
words we use, is a question which Descartes was more willing to ask of the words
of the scholastics for which he had much
contempt than of the words of his own
philosophy. What he took to stand for
simple natures "thought", "extension", "existence," all were to be subject to the
criticism of his successors. Leibniz at-
tacked the notion of extension and reduced
it to one of the relational complexes
which, being multiplex, could not be ul-
timately real. Leibniz himself, of course,
had his own favorite simple characteristics, but his critique of those of Descartes
were effective.

Locke made the ideas any objects of
the mind when it thinks and he, too, de-
pended as much on the suggestion of
language as on the revelations of introspec-
tion. It is well known that the British critics
of both Locke and Descartes exploited this
point. Both Berkeley and Hume insist
that the misleading suggestions of speech
must be resisted. And Berkeley's critique

of the language of general terms repeats
many of the nominalist arguments of the
fourteenth century against abstraction and
the alleged progeny with which it tries
to multiply concepts in the consciousness.

Recent philosophical discussion about
concepts is too complex to be discussed
in any detail here, but some suggestion
about the role of modern logic should be
made. Modern formal logic in the first
place has several different forms, but the
most influential of them comes essentially
from the work of Peirce, Frege, and Russell. In this form predicates do the entire
work of description, and the logical constants, i.e. connectives, quantifiers, and
copula, are assigned special symbols.

One of the most extraordinary results
of the use of this formalism was achieved
by Russell in the *Principia Mathematica*
(Vol. I, 14) in which he showed that sentences with grammatical subjects of the
form "The so-and-so" (with "the" in the
singular) can be replaced by sentences
without such grammatical subjects. The

philosophical significance of this for the doctrine of concepts is, briefly, as follows.

Russell held that if singular descriptive phrases could be thus eliminated, the descriptive phrase had no independent context-free meaning. Hence, the search for a single concept which would be the intra-psychic non-verbal counterpart of, for example, "the present King of France" would be vain. But the construction of indefinite descriptions had the same effect. In a sentence such as "John rode a horse", "a horse" is not to have an independent meaning. Consequently, in "John thought of a horse," is not to be analysed into "John", "thought of," and "a horse." Hence, there is not to be some referent or other in every case corresponding to the grammatical subjects and objects of sentences, and so no need for a concept corresponding to these experiences.

There are difficulties with this way of dealing with the substantives of ordinary speech, and they have not been resolved to the satisfaction of a working majority of philosophers. But the alternative theories that have been offered do not encourage a return to the classical doctrines.

Moreover, modern logic has shown how many expressions, which at one time were supposed to require special concepts in order to be understood at all, can be so defined that conceptual counterparts could not be assumed to exist. This would be true, for example, of the numerals of arithmetic, and the geometrical expressions of pure geometry.

Now it is to be admitted that many expressions of the sciences and even of ordinary discourse, e.g. "table", "house", "dog," etc., cannot be given explicit definitions which are adequate. Of course, there is some debate about this, but the weight of expert opinion seems to be that explicit definitions of these expressions cannot be provided. But, again, the alternatives do not suggest a return to the classical doctrines.

As I said at the beginning of this discussion, I have not wished to deny that there are contents of consciousness which are not reducible to anything radically

different from themselves. This admission
or insistence, however, does not mean that
concepts or ideas in the sense in which
those terms were used in the traditional
philosophers will have much chance of
explaining the meanings of substantive expressions or the way in which the mind
succeeds in understanding the world. For
the conditions which have to be met in
order to use concepts or ideas appear to
be incompatible with the way in which
knowledge is acquired and inconsistent
with any defensible theory of the meaning of expressions used to describe and
explain the world.

The Aquinas Lectures

Published by the Marquette University Press
Milwaukee, Wisconsin 53233

St. Thomas and the Life of Learning (1937) by
John F. McCormick, S.J., (1874-1943) professor of philosophy, Loyola University.

sbn 87462-101-1

St. Thomas and the Gentiles (1938) by Morti-
mer J. Adler, Ph.D., director of the Institute of
Philosophical Research, San Francisco, Calif.

sbn 87462-102-X

St. Thomas and the Greeks (1939) by Anton C.
Pegis, Ph.D., professor of philosophy, Pontifical Institute of Mediaeval Studies, Toronto.

sbn 87462-103-8

The Nature and Functions of Authority (1940)
by Yves Simon, Ph.D., (1903-1961) professor
of philosophy of social thought, University of
Chicago.   sbn 87462-104-6

St. Thomas and Analogy (1941) by Gerald B.
Phelan, Ph.D., (1892-1965) professor of philosophy, St. Michael's College, Toronto.

sbn 87462-105-4

St. Thomas and the Problem of Evil (1942) by
Jacques Maritain, Ph.D., professor *emeritus*
of philosophy, Princeton University.

sbn 87462-106-2

Humanism and Theology (1943) by Werner Jaeger, Ph.D., Litt.D., (1888-1961) University professor, Harvard University. sbn 87462-107-0

The Nature and Origins of Scientism (1944) by John Wellmuth. sbn 87462-108-9

Cicero in the Courtroom of St. Thomas Aquinas (1945) by E. K. Rand, Ph.D., Litt.D., LL.D., (1871-1945) Pope professor of Latin, *emeritus,* Harvard University. sbn 87462-109-7

St. Thomas and Epistemology (1946) by Louis-Marie Regis, O.P., Th.L., Ph.D., director of the Albert the Great Institute of Mediaeval Studies, University of Montreal.

sbn 87462-110-0

St. Thomas and the Greek Moralists (1947, Spring) by Vernon J. Bourke, Ph.D., professor of philosophy, St. Louis University, St. Louis, Missouri. sbn 87462-111-9

History of Philosophy and Philosophical Education (1947, Fall) by Étienne Gilson of the *Académie française,* director of studies and professor of the history of Mediaeval philosophy, Pontifical Institute of Mediaeval Studies, Toronto. sbn 87462-112-7

The Natural Desire for God (1948) by William R. O'Connor, S.T.L., Ph.D., former professor of dogmatic theology, St. Joseph's Seminary, Dunwoodie, N.Y. sbn 87462-113-5

St. Thomas and the World State (1949) by Robert M. Hutchins, former Chancellor of the University of Chicago, president of the Fund for the Republic. sbn 87462-114-3

Method in Metaphysics (1950) by Robert J. Henle, S.J., Ph.D., academic vice-president, St. Louis University, St. Louis, Missouri.
sbn 87462-115-1

Wisdom and Love in St. Thomas Aquinas (1951) by Étienne Gilson of the *Académie française*, director of studies and professor of the history of Mediaeval philosophy, Pontifical Institute of Mediaeval Studies, Toronto.
sbn 87462-116-X

The Good in Existential Metaphysics (1952) by Elizabeth G. Salmon, Ph.D., professor of philosophy in the graduate school, Fordham University. sbn 87462-117-8

St. Thomas and the Object of Geometry (1953) by Vincent Edward Smith, Ph.D., director, Philosophy of Science Institute, St. John's University. sbn 87462-118-6

Realism and Nominalism Revisited (1954) by Henry Veatch, Ph.D., professor and chairman of the department of philosophy, Northwestern University. sbn 87462-119-4

Imprudence in St. Thomas Aquinas (1955) by Charles J. O'Neil, Ph.D., professor of philosophy, Villanova University. sbn 87462-120-8

The Truth That Frees (1956) by Gerard Smith, S.J., Ph.D., professor of philosophy, Marquette University. sbn 87462-121-6

St. Thomas and the Future of Metaphysics (1957) by Joseph Owens, C.Ss.R., Ph.D., professor of philosophy, Pontifical Institute of Mediaeval Studies, Toronto. sbn 87462-122-4

Thomas and the Physics of 1958: A Confrontation (1958) by Henry Margenau, Ph.D., Eugene Higgins professor of physics and natural philosophy, Yale University.
sbn 87462-123-2

Metaphysics and Ideology (1959) by Wm. Oliver Martin, Ph.D., professor of philosophy, University of Rhode Island. sbn 87462-124-0

Language, Truth and Poetry (1960) by Victor M. Hamm, Ph.D., professor of English, Marquette University. sbn 87462-125-9

Metaphysics and Historicity (1961) by Emil L. Fackenheim, Ph.D., professor of philosophy, University of Toronto. sbn 87462-126-7

The Lure of Wisdom (1962) by James D. Collins, Ph.D., professor of philosophy, St. Louis University. sbn 87462-127-5

Religion and Art (1963) by Paul Weiss, Ph.D. Sterling professor of philosophy, Yale University. sbn 87462-128-3

St. Thomas and Philosophy (1964) by Anton C. Pegis, Ph.D., professor of philosophy, Pontifical Institute of Mediaeval Studies, Toronto.

SBN 87462-129-1

The University In Process (1965) by John O. Riedl, Ph.D., dean of faculty, Queensboro Community College.

SBN 87462-130-5

The Pragmatic Meaning of God (1966) by Robert O. Johann, associate professor of philosophy, Fordham University.

SBN 87462-131-3

Religion and Empiricism (1967) by John E. Smith, Ph.D., professor of philosophy, Yale University.

SBN 87462-132-1

The Subject (1968) by Bernard Lonergan, S.J., S.T.D., professor of Dogmatic Theory, Regis College, Ontario and Gregorian University, Rome.

SBN 87462-133-X

Beyond Trinity (1969) by Bernard J. Cooke, S.T.D.

SBN 87462-134-8

Uniform format, cover and binding.